Shopify

Build a Six-Figure Business Using Shopify & Aliexpress

Table of Contents

Introduction 3

Part 1 – Research 7

Part 2 – Building your business 10

Chapter 2 – Uploading products 12

Chapter 3 – Setting store collections, tags, and other groups
.... 14

Part 3 – Marketing on facebook 16

Part 4 – Processing your orders 21

Conclusion 26

Introduction

I want to thank you and congratulate you for purchasing the book, *"Shopify – Build a Six-Figure Business Using Shopify & Aliexpress"*.

Shopify is an online platform that allows you to start your own venture by selling the products and sending each item at the doorsteps of the buyers. The main purpose of sharing this piece of content with you is to build your own Shopify store by choosing the particular niches. It is quite simple if you follow all the shared steps for building your personal store. The selection of niche is very important as you must know about your targeted audience. Make sure that your chosen niche doesn't have few range of expensive products.

Then, you have to outsource the products from some suggested online websites. this is an e-commerce site that helps you outsource the items and then sell them with the certain profit margin.

Make a purchase from such stores by placing an order. Then, send the items to the respective home addresses through shipping. It is a quite profitable business that can be started from home without any investment. You can open your own online shopping store and develop the best way of making large profits without any trouble. There are few issues that you'd have to address before starting this business. You must share the picture of the item that you can send exactly what has been shown. Otherwise, it may end up by losing the customers, and they also raise many questions. You can be able to add as many products on your page as you can on the store.

There are many benefits of building your own Shopify store. Firstly, it is an opportunity to earn as much profit as you can without any restrictions. You can get many orders and earn a lot without investing a cent. Isn't it amazing? You'd find a great chance to buy and share products with the customers. The best thing about choosing Shopify is the trust of people on this platform. There are no doubts or confusions in the minds of existing users of this source (as a small business store). It is hard to find such beneficial e-commerce site that has already changed many lives by taking their venture to the next level. The site's developers don't leave any stone unturned to give you a successful business by offering plenty of great features. The marketing, customer support, add-ons and many other conveniences help to stick to this platform. Once you create an account here, you won't want to switch to any other option ever. The long-term monetary benefits are guaranteed by relying on this e-commerce site.

© **Copyright 2016 by Steve Goldman- All rights reserved.**

This document is geared towards providing exact and reliable information in regards to the topic and issue covered. The publication is sold with the idea that the publisher is not required to render accounting, officially permitted, or otherwise, qualified services. If advice is necessary, legal or professional, a practiced individual in the profession should be ordered.

- From a Declaration of Principles which was accepted and approved equally by a Committee of the American Bar Association and a Committee of Publishers and Associations.

In no way is it legal to reproduce, duplicate, or transmit any part of this document in either electronic means or in printed format. Recording of this publication is strictly prohibited and any storage of this document is not allowed unless with written permission from the publisher. All rights reserved.

The information provided herein is stated to be truthful and consistent, in that any liability, in terms of inattention or otherwise, by any usage or abuse of any policies, processes, or directions contained within is the solitary and utter responsibility of the recipient reader. Under no circumstances will any legal responsibility or blame be held against the publisher for any reparation, damages, or monetary loss due to the information herein, either directly or indirectly.

Respective authors own all copyrights not held by the publisher.

The information herein is offered for informational purposes solely, and is universal as so. The presentation of the information is without contract or any type of guarantee assurance.

The trademarks that are used are without any consent, and the publication of the trademark is without permission or backing by the trademark owner. All trademarks and brands within this book are for clarifying purposes only and are the owned by the owners themselves, not affiliated with this document.

Part 1 – Research

1) Profitability sellable online is the way of earning profits by selling different products through internet medium. It is the way that allows an individual or team of people to sell the items by communicating with interested customers through the internet. There can be many items that you can sell online, and each of these turns into sellable stuff for the sake of profitability.

2) The wanelo.com and amazon.com offer a wide range of hot items. These are established online sources of shopping. You can easily get access to the items through reaching different categories. These categories are available to search the desired products within few seconds or minutes.

3) We are going to use supplies related to the wearable of women. The women stuff is based on clothing, jewelry, and footwear. All the supplies related to such items would be purchased from amazon, eBay, home depot and aliexpress.com. The research process is time-taking and requires lots of work to be completed.

4) We are targeting for the price range that starts from 1 USD to 100 USD. The items would have prices within the given range. None of any item would be available with the price higher than 100 USD.

5) We are going to sell to the women as they are our targeted audience. The niche which you'd choose

is based on Women's Fashion and Clothing. Then the process of building a store for this niche would be started. It is quite simple to do through outsourcing respective items from reliable sources i.e. Amazon, Aliexpress, and eBay.

Guide for Choosing the Products or Niche

The customers vary from each other with many aspects. For instance, people with higher incomes don't prefer buying anything online while mid-income earners spend a lot in buying small items frequently. Although, it doesn't happen all the time but the strange possibility (which has been seen a lot so far).

Your business can reach the heights of success by choosing the right demographic. It can become valuable by choosing the good clients. There are many people who can spend a lot only to fulfill their desires. These are known as hobbyists who don't feel any reluctance to buy expensive items just to meet their dreams. For example, many people the smartphone freaks spend a lot if prices more than their laptops and other gadgets as per their hobby.

There is a price-sensitive lot of buyers known as business clients. Unlike individual buyers, they purchase items in bulk and help the sellers to generate higher profits more quickly than selling items to traditional buyers. The long-term high-volume relationship can be developed by earning their trust and establishing a good rapport. However, the sellers need to attract both types of purchasers to gain more monetary benefits.

The loyal customers or repeat buyers are those who become a permanent or long-term source of generating profits for the businesses. They buy the items frequently due to the trust on the seller. These type of customers are proved to be highly beneficial for the businesses from monetary perspectives.

Part 2 – Building your business

Chapter 1 – Setting your Shopify store

Setting up the store of Shopify isn't a complex thing to do. Anyone can open the store if h/she is capable enough to outsource items and selling them by living up to the expectations of buyers. This kind of shopping provides great convenience to the buyers by receiving the desired items at their doorsteps. Have a look at the simple process of opening an account on Shopify.

1) The initial stage of starting your Shopify venture is to create an account. Literally, this is so simple. You need to sign up to the given source on the website and follow the instructions accordingly.

2) The next process is to choose a payment option to get money from the buyers through online. Few reliable payment sources are Paypal, Skrill, etc. However, it is your choice to select the payment options as per convenience for instant transfer of money.

3) The third process is about setting up shipping options. There, you have to develop the whole setup for making the shipping process convenient and easier. Always make sure to make the timely delivery to force buyers for making frequent purchases.

4) Next process is to choose a theme for your page. This must grab the attention of visitors and interested buyers. it is a human psyche that few colors on web

page never appeal the visitors and they also judge the credibility of the seller and the available stuff.

Chapter 2 – Uploading products

The major process is based on uploading the products through aliexpress.com. It is very time-taking and attention-seeking procedure that can only be done once you do thorough research. First of all, you would have to save the links of products and keep all of them on record. It is a useful suggestion to avoid missing any product. Have a look at few steps based on details of the uploading procedure.

1) First of all, you need to copy the pictures from aliexpress.com. Then, paste them directly on your Shopify store or keep a record of products details along with their images for uploading later. Make sure that you download the picture and then upload it to the store. Never try to save the small image for uploading it on your page. Customers always check the products by zooming in their pictures and then they make a final purchase decision.

2) The descriptions of products need to be copied by paying full attention. Make sure that you copy every detail so that customers get to know everything about the product. Unlike images, you can copy the text and paste it on Shopify's page. It is suggested to read the description before posting it on your source. Sometimes, the irrelevant info is also shared mistakenly that creates a lot of trouble for the business owners. Never try to add additional false information. You must know that the product would be bought by people any the truth can be easily unveiled in front of them. The key to a successful online shopping store is to

share the actual specifications and images of the products.

3) The product identifiers or search results are best to add in Shopify's page. All of the reliable and good shopping sites provide the best product searching sections so that buyers can find desired products without any hassle. This is the way that plays an important role in retaining buyers. The interested customers love to have instant search results and save time on finding products. Remember that if your page doesn't have a product identifier based on quick searching, then forget about making a successful Shopify store. The visitors must be able to get instant results and access to the desired products within few seconds. There is no shortcut to making your online store successful other than spending several months and putting a lot of effort.

Chapter 3 – Setting store collections, tags, and other groups

All the products available on the store must be placed in an organized way. Every item should be placed in their specific category's page. Setting up the store's collection is another burdensome task. However, if you do it with the proper planning, then everything would go well. Instead of creating a mess of products on the page, you will have to follow the shared guide for organizing the collection in a proper way.

Group the Items

Make certain groups or categories of the items. For example, we've chosen the women's fashion and clothing category. So, all of the items related to this category would be shown together. The clothing items will be displayed together like the jewelry and accessories. Grouping of items tells the actual way of displaying every item without creating a mess on the page. It is also helpful for buyers to find the related stuff without multiple clicks or searching here and there.

Tagging

Tagging is the best feature that helps to relate similar products. In this way, the buyers can also see the suggestions of same products. This helps the store owners to get more buyers too as tagging widen the search of products by relating the items together. For example, if one has typed the keyword "ABC Pants", then the related items (like ABC T-shirts) would also be added to search results and even on the page.

Building Store Categories

The categories are developed to separate the items from each other. For example, there would be different categories of clothing, accessories, jewelry and footwear. These categories would help buyers to choose the products that lie under each category without any hassle. Just imagine the outlook of your store if it is cluttered with the jewelry, accessories, clothing, and footwear at one page. Adding categories has become quite important these days. The inconvenience of searching products is the major reason of losing buyers. Categories of different items make it simple for the buyers to see, pick and place an order.

Part 3 – Marketing on facebook

Promoting or advertising any business is ideal through social networking platforms. Among many of the social media sources, facebook is considered as a most useful platform for marketing of any business. This clearly shows that you must only rely on this platform for promoting any kind of business. Your newly-developed Shopify store can also be promoted on facebook in a great way. Make you facebook channel (that should be attractive) and invite people to get likes. With the constant increase in likes, the more people would know about your products. Secondly, the sharing icon isn't less than a blessing as one share allow the product to be introduced in front of more new people.

Run Facebook Ads

Running the facebook ads for any kind of business is not complex at all. Facebook Inc requires a minimal fee for suggesting your page for more likes to different profiles. The more effective way is to make short videos or images (with descriptions) and spread them as much as you can. The facebook team would send you a procedure for making payment and activation of ads. All you need to do is to take full advantage of this opportunity and never miss any chance to share the ads with a big lot of facebook users.

Choose the Target Audience

As we've supposed the niche of Women's fashion and clothing, then the targeted audience would be the females with different age groups. Most of the females who make shopping of stuff from shared categories lie in the ages between 16 to 55 years. If you've chosen any other niche, then it's necessary to make through research for choosing your target audience. The hack of grabbing the attention of more people for a single niche is to show benefits of the offered products for people other than your major targeted audience as well. For example, your target audience for beauty products can be men as well. These days, males are also concerned about their face complexion, dark circles, and spot. So, why won't you get the advantage of it by mentioning benefits of beauty products also for the males?

The Budget

Budget plays a basic role to push the venture for proceeding further. if you've nothing to spend, then none of any trick would be workable for investing in the store. As we've started running the Women's Fashion Store based on other related things as well. The budget in opening a Shopify store is equal to nothing indeed. All you need to do is to buy the products from the available sources i.e. aliexpress.com, amazon.com and others, etc. these stores are reliable and deliver the products on time. Therefore, we would give the delivery time of a week to our customers and then place an order for receiving the stuff. After receiving the items, the next stage would be to do some additional packaging of the items, and then these would be ready for shipping. The shipping process is a major phase that needs to be done properly. Send all the items with the proper care and never make any mistake in the packaging. In the beginning, it is better to start by investing a small amount of budget. Otherwise, it would be very tough to compensate the cost.

How to scale the ads on facebook?

There is a simple process of scaling facebook ads. Running paid traffic has the hardest part that is called scaling. You can run a good facebook campaign to generate 500 leads if it is easy to find the target market. However, there is also a possibility of generating 5,000 to 50,000 leads at once by relying on some best tricks. Before you start to notice fatigue, you can only target the same group of people. It is drop-dead easy to breathe life into your campaigns for volume. The profitable scaling of facebook ads and campaigns is to use a tool that works like a miracle.

If you're not putting your ads in front of the right audience, no matter how captivating your copy and image but the campaign will result in failure. Finding the target audience by using the workable tool was considered as a bothersome task. However, you can do it once checking the proper usage of tools. By advertising and locating to audiences, there is a process that will show you how to scale your campaigns.

A good tool gives data to find where else your target market is hanging out on the facebook. If you've already a success with one of your ad sets. There is a tool that provides you the opportunity to unveil behavioral and demographic data before targeting it with the advertisement has been released by facebook recently called "Audience Insights". This tool is quite workable and works like magic for scaling of ads on facebook. You can't find such great tool from any source on internet. The best thing about this tool is to perform the steps without making any issue. You would be able to make research on the custom audiences as this tool allows the users for doing it in a great manner.

These are custom phone lists, website visitors, and email lists. A user can also be able to target data through influencers in the specific niche and FB pages of competitors. To explore the page which your audience is likely to prefer is possible through leveraging facebook's data. It also supports to search the individuals identical to like your fan page and converted on your web pages. The use of Audience Insight can be quite beneficial for you to grab more attention of buyers towards your business.

Get Rid of Items That Won't be Sold Out

It happens many times with the store owners to keep a stock of some items which never be sold out.it is better to waste your money on such things, you should have some knowledge about what to offer and what to reject. Otherwise, your new venture would be on a stake in the beginning. It happens a lot that the most demanding items in the current period tend to lose their popularity after a small span.

This is the major reason that takes the owners into trouble when they see that product is losing their demands. The through research about the products and choosing those that have consistent popularity are the key secrets for a successful venture. If you will simply fill out your Shopify store with loads of products without paying attention to them, then nobody would stop your venture to end with a lot of losses.

The items that don't worth a lot must be avoided to add in the product's list of your Shopify webpage. It is also best to get suggestions from the successful owners of the shopify store. It would be very helpful to proceed further. in case if you've bought the items that are less likely to be sold anytime soon, then the best way is to use cost leadership strategy for ending their stock. This is the best strategy to sell the items that are low in demand. You simply have to make their availability possible by reducing half of your profit margin from the products.

For example, if you're getting the profit of $0.5 in a product, then reduce it to the $0.25. It would give you benefit as well as help to end the stock without any trouble. There are more ways to get rid of the items that are hard to sell or face a drastic change in demand. It is highly suggested that products that are bought rarely or aren't used a lot by people must have less stock. For instance, the jerseys are high in demand in the winter season. You need to buy them in a limited stock to avoid any losses in the future. If the stock remains available for the start of summer, then it will become more difficult to clear the inventory from te store.

Part 4 – Processing your orders

The last and most important stage of online shopping are to deliver the required items with proper care and on time. It is called the processing of orders that starts from receiving the items from a vendor and then prepare them to send to the place of buyers. This procedure requires a lot of attention because you've responsibility to deliver items in good condition. These must not have any defects or broken from any side. When you buy the stock of any product, make sure that all the items are in good condition. Never try to pack the stuff without checking them properly. After the through examination, you can proceed further to start packaging of the products.

The products need to be wrapped perfectly so that neither of these will be broken nor have any damages. After the complete packaging of the products, the procedure adding addresses on each item actually begins. This is also a time-taking step that requires a lot of attention. There is no chance of making any mistake as delivery of a right item on right time is necessary for sure. Otherwise, you'd have to face a lot of trouble that results in losing customers as well. Each item must have the sticker of your firm's name so that customer never forget to place the order again and again.

Order placement

Your Shopify store's web page must have good options for quick order placement. The best process of placing an order is to click on the 'Add to Cart' icon, mark the field to agree by showing agreement to the prices and delivery charges. After clicking on the 'Place an Order' icon, the order is finalized for the starting the next processes. Make sure that you make this procedure quite simple and convenient for the buyers. The best suggestion is to keep in touch with the buyers from start to the end. This action really grab the attention of the buyers, and they think to select you again for future orders. The customers of our Women's Fashion Store would have the option to place multiple orders without any hassle. The process would be comprised of few simple steps that hardly take a minute for single order placement.

Sending The Orders

The sending of orders is based on transferring the items through any chosen courier service. Make sure that the service is reliable and would deliver the orders on time. You'd also have to deal with the courier services company for regular delivery of a certain amount of items. All you need to do is to send the orders to the courier company on time. Also, get the assurance of delivering the items on time. However, stay in touch with the buyers as well to get confirmation about who have received and who haven't yet. Once you transfer all the items to the courier company, then the job of senders would start. For example, if the two dresses have been ordered by a client, then we would send them both to the courier company for taking the package to the buyer's home.

The Delivery:

The delivery of items is all about sending the stuff without any damage to the buyer's place. Once the buyer gets the item in hands and pay for it, one of your order's delivery comes to an end. Then, the same procedure is required to be performed again, and the process goes on. Once a buyer pays for the order received from our Women's fashion store, we would proceed further to send more orders to the other customers. The customers always want delivery of the products on time. The late deliveries pay a really bad impression on them. Therefore, your store must be capable of delivering the products without making any delays. The delivery of items is based on three different stages. First of all, the items are prepared for packaging. Then, all the orders are sent to the courier service company. The third step is to take the orders to the home.

Benefits of Choosing Shopify

It is true that there are numerous options for creating online stores on the web. However, few of them are worthwhile and provide innumerable benefits (profit). Shopify is the platform where you won't only get the opportunity to offer plenty of products but also get a quick response and lots of traffic in a very short span of time. Have a look at few great benefits of choosing Shopify as your final choice for creating an online store.

- There is no need to save a lot of investments. This is the best platform that gives you the opportunity to start from zero. Neither you need to spend a dollar on creating Shopify's account, nor you'd have to make a lot of effort as well. This shows that the money would begin to come instead of getting wasted on your side. Save and get a lot is the best policy of the developers of Shopify. This benefit actually gives you a lot without putting your money on a stake as people do in starting traditional ventures.

- There is no limit of adding products in different categories. This is really great opportunity to offer a variety of items and get more chances of earning as well. This is actually a worthwhile benefit but doesn't mean that you start adding plenty of items right after opening the account. It is better to add few products initially that you can buy and deliver without any hassle. The advantage of the uncountable addition of products is for the established Shopify stores.

- The user interface is quite simple of the Shopify store. All you need to do is to create an account and let's begin adding products. You won't have to hire web experts for the development of product searching section or placement of icons in a proper way. It's simply like a served opportunity that only bother you to invite people for being your buyers.

- The products of almost all types of niches can be sold in the Shopify store. You won't have to think twice before selecting any niche. Don't feel any reluctance or fear of refusal of any niche. You can sell everything except few illegal items that would be mentioned in the policy and rules section. This is as simple as millions of people use this platform for selling the items from selected niches.

- The trusted, and top-rated platform is the best place to sell the products. You can't get such wonderful chance of starting a venture without large investments. Secondly, there is a guarantee of immediate success in the business for long-term. Your store of Shopify can reach the heights of success in a very short period. It's better to rely on this platform if you're damn serious about starting a new venture in the form of an online store.

- Shopify is an e-commerce site that offers the best security and inbuilt speed for hosting. Every user has dual needs from their chosen e-commerce platform for running an online store. It becomes highly beneficial for the owners to provide quick loading their online stores. In this way, the instant search makes buyers feel great, and they don't decide to switch to other option.

- All of the important features are offered by Shopify to make the creation of an online store easier for you. Many add-ons are available to make every option easier to visit and understand for the page visitors. However, all the add-ons are not free of cost. For instance, an email marketing company called MailChimp is linked with Shopify in the form of add-on. It really works great for marketing your online store.

- The designs of the page are also available in large variety. Secondly, there are best marketing options to promote your Shopify store in the shortest possible time. You probably fail to get such awesome designs by relying on any other store.

- The customer support is excellent that only deserve a lot of praises. You can get quick responses to all the queries through live chat or email. All the queries and complaints are responded in the less possible time so that customers don't have to wait a lot. The phone support, email, chat, FAQs and some other mediums are available for providing excellent support to the customers.

Conclusion

Shopify is the fun using e-commerce platform for making your dream come true related to starting a home business. It requires nothing except to sign up for a site. Follow the instructions and add the products. Then, you can also be able to outsource the items for selling to the customers by getting some profit.

Thank you again for purchasing this book!

I hope this book was able to help you to open your personal online store from a trusted source. The best thing about starting your Shopify store is guaranteed to generate lots of profits within few months. There is no need for any investments to make thousands of dollars in a day. This reliable platform is hard to find anywhere on the web. This book is a detailed guide to beginning your small venture with the support of a well-known e-commerce site. You can't disbelieve on this online platform as the reviews and ratings show the evidence of its credibility. Best of luck for your future online store of Shopify.

The next step is to simply create a Shopify account and become an entrepreneur.

Finally, if you enjoyed this book, then I'd like to ask you for a favor, would you be kind enough to leave a review for this book on Amazon? It'd be greatly appreciated!

www.ingramcontent.com/pod-product-compliance
Lightning Source LLC
Chambersburg PA
CBHW070720210526
45170CB00021B/1382